EXTRAORDINARY WILD WEATHER

Contents

The World's Wildest Weather

Look out of your window. Weather is what's happening outside — and it can change before your eyes. Sunny weather quickly turns to clouds or rain. In some parts of the world, you could even be in for really wild weather, such as scorching heat, bitter blizzards, or floods.

 Every year, around 1,000 tornadoes spin their way through the Midwest. These terrifying, twisting columns of air appear out of nowhere and can tear apart a town.

Hot, Cold, or Mild

Climate is different from weather. Climate is the type of weather an area usually has each year. The sun shines strongest in the tropics, the areas near the equator — an imaginary line around the earth. The tropics have a hot climate. The Antarctic and Arctic have less sunshine, so they have cold climates. The areas in between have mild climates.

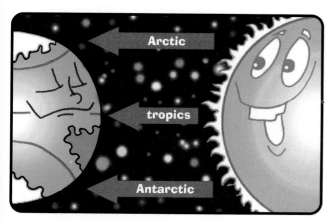

Changes, Changes

The seasons are changes in the weather that happen regularly throughout a year. In areas where the weather is mild, there are four seasons. Winter is cold. In spring, days become brighter. Summer is warm, then cooler weather returns each fall.

Wild World

Which parts of the world have the wildest weather of all? Check out some top wild weather spots on the map below.

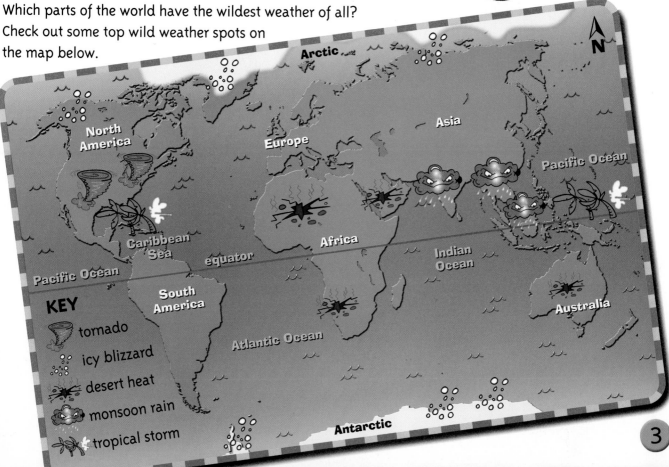

KEY

- tornado
- icy blizzard
- desert heat
- monsoon rain
- tropical storm

What Makes Weather?

You know what weather looks like, but where does all that sunshine and rain come from? Where does snow start? Why do deadly storms brew? The answers lie high up in the sky.

Wrapped in Air

Weather happens in the atmosphere — a layer of air wrapped around our planet. Almost all our weather happens in the lowest part of the atmosphere, called the *troposphere*. It's like a gigantic mixer, churning up all the ingredients to make different types of weather.

It's cozy in here!

That's Weird!

Earth is warming up. Heat that normally escapes into space is getting trapped in the atmosphere. This has caused 75 percent of the ice on Mount Kilimanjaro in Africa to melt in fewer than 100 years. That means its ice may all be gone by the year 2020!

Here is a hurricane seen from space. This huge, spinning storm is hovering over the coast of Central America.

What
causes weather?

What a lovely day!

Sunshine, air, and water mix together to make different kinds of weather. For instance, when sunshine and air mix, the days are warm and sunny.

warm air

cool air

Hold on to your hat!

When air warms up, it becomes lighter and rises. Cooler, heavier air rushes in to take its place and makes windy weather.

Here comes the rain!

water vapor

SEA

Sunshine turns water in seas, lakes, and rivers into a gas called water vapor. The vapor forms clouds. Then snow and rain fall.

Flash, Bang, Boom!

Lightning shoots out of a cloud, looking for the fastest route to the ground. It heads for the tallest thing around, zooms straight through it, and down into the earth. Usually, a skyscraper or tall tree gets zapped, but if you're really unlucky, it could be you!

Where Does Lightning Come From?

Lightning is made inside a huge, dark storm cloud, called a cumulonimbus. Inside a storm cloud, water droplets and ice crystals rub together. This rubbing makes electricity, which builds up and builds up. Suddenly, it surges out of the cloud in the huge spark that we call lightning.

There's a spark between us!

And Thunder?

Thunder is made by lightning. A lightning bolt is amazingly hot — four times hotter than the surface of the sun. Air around the bolt heats up so quickly that it expands with a mighty rumble. This creates a massive roll of thunder.

BOOM!

Why the flash before the boom?

① Why do you see lightning before you hear thunder? Thunder and lightning set off together. But light travels so fast that lightning speeds off.

② Sound travels more slowly than light, so thunder lags behind. It takes five seconds for sound to travel a mile (three seconds for one kilometer).

③ Here comes the winner! Lightning always arrives first. This is why you see the flash of lightning before you hear the boom of thunder.

Time to Run?

Light travels faster than sound, so it's easy to figure out how far away a thunderstorm is from you. When you see the lightning flash, start counting the seconds until you hear the thunderclap. Divide the number of seconds by five to find out how many miles away the storm is. (Divide by three to work this out in kilometers.)

1–2–3–4–5 Five seconds. So the storm is one mile away!

TRUE STORY!

Lightning can kill you, but some people are lucky. One park ranger in Virginia was hit by lightning seven times! He lost his eyebrows and the nail on his big toe, and his hair was set on fire. But he survived to tell the tale!

A bolt of lightning strikes a tree. Lightning is so hot that it often sets trees on fire.

It's a Washout
(or Who Left the Tap on?)

Imagine floodwater gushing past your home, washing away belongings, cars, houses, and trees. Floods usually happen when it rains very hard. There's too much water on the land for the soil to soak up. Rivers can't carry the water away fast enough, so they overflow their banks.

EXTRA! EXTRA!
The cost of flood damage in the U.S.A. over the last 10 years is enough to buy half the people on the planet an umbrella!

HA HA

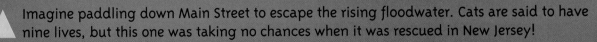
Imagine paddling down Main Street to escape the rising floodwater. Cats are said to have nine lives, but this one was taking no chances when it was rescued in New Jersey!

Wow!

The most flooded area on Earth is the land around the Huang He River in China. This river has burst its banks a record-breaking 1,500 times in 3,500 years. So every two to three years, people put up with flooded homes and ruined crops.

We can't go on meeting like this!

Good Floods

Time for dinner!

If you were an animal living in the Pantanal wetlands in Brazil, you'd think floods were great. When the Amazon River floods, it brings water to dry land. This makes the soil rich and provides plenty of food for the huge variety of wildlife there.

Mud, Mud, and More Mud

Floodwater makes land soggy and heavy. On a slope, wet soil can slip downhill, causing a devastating landslide of mud and rocks. The mud sweeps everything along in its path, burying cars and houses and seeping into every nook and cranny.

Where
do floods come from?

Slow-moving bands of clouds that produce heavy rain are often to blame for floods. They make it rain for days and days.

On hills and mountains, snow can melt quickly after heavy snowfall. Then rivers overflow and flooding can occur.

Violent storms off the coast can batter the shore with huge waves. The sea invades the land, which causes flooding.

Wet! Wet! Wet!

Most thunderstorms last for an hour or two, but imagine what it's like living in a place where heavy rain falls for days on end. A quarter of the world's population puts up with weather like this every year — it's called the monsoon season.

It's the season...

Monsoons happen in the tropics — the areas of the world near the equator. Here, there are two seasons — a cool, dry season, and a hot, wet season. During the wet season, air rises over the warm land, drawing in a moist wind from the ocean. This wind, called the monsoon, makes a steady stream of clouds and rain over the land.

Map of India

The traffic battles bravely through floodwater during the monsoon. Day after day of rain causes the drains to overflow and the water in the street to become very high.

...to celebrate!

After a blisteringly hot summer, the rain brought by the monsoon wind is a welcome relief. The dry, dusty fields receive water and crops grow. In some parts of India, people welcome the monsoon with a festival called Teej. Women and girls, dressed in their traditional clothes, sing and dance. Elephants draped with colorful silks have their trunks and tusks decorated, then march in a procession.

Humongous Hurricanes

Hurricanes are one of the most spectacular weather phenomena. These massive, spinning storms tear across oceans, heading for the shore where they create total havoc.

EXTRA! EXTRA!
Hurricane is a Caribbean word meaning "big wind." In the Pacific, hurricanes are called typhoons, and in Australia they're known as willy-willies.

  This may look like a junkyard, but a short while ago, it was a trailer park. A violent hurricane has wrecked the place, tossing things in the air and tearing people's homes apart.

How to Make a Hurricane

1 A hurricane starts at sea when the water temperature is more than 80°F (27°C). A group of thunderstorms draws warm, moist air from the ocean's surface.

2 The thunderstorms grow and swirl around in a circle. As they spin faster, they form one huge storm. The storm turns into a menacing hurricane.

3 A hurricane races across the ocean, whipping up waves that are enormous enough to sink a ship. While a hurricane remains at sea, it is at its most vicious.

What's the Damage?

A hurricane makes winds of up to 190 miles per hour (300 kmh). When it hits land it starts to fade away, but it still spells big trouble. Huge waves crash against the shore, buildings are smashed, and trees are uprooted. Boats, planes, and cars are picked up and scattered like toys.

Wow!

In the middle of a hurricane there is a hole called the eye, which is around 20–30 miles (30–50 km) wide. Inside the eye, all is strangely calm. Tropical birds sometimes travel in a hurricane's eye and end up safe, far from home!

Tornado Terrors

A tornado, or twister, is a spinning column of air that sucks up everything in its path. During thunderstorms, hot air rises and meets cold air. If the air currents whirl around each other, then a deadly twister is born!

Tornado Alley

Anyone living in the U.S.A. between Texas and Illinois can expect an average of 750 twisters a year. Welcome to Tornado Alley! Most tornadoes cause minor damage in the countryside, but when they hit a town they toss people, cars, and even buildings high into the air. In 1925, a tornado in Missouri wrecked four towns.

Tornado Ride

1 It's rumored that 13 Chinese schoolchildren were sucked up by a tornado in 1986. It was said to have carried them 12 miles (19 km) before it ran out of steam.

2 The tornado dumped the children back on the ground. Amazingly, no one was hurt, although a few had lost their hats!

That's Weird!

A tornado on a sea or lake is called a waterspout. It's a twisting column of spray and water vapor that sways over the waves like a snake. Sailors in ancient times thought that waterspouts were sea monsters who had come to devour their ships.

Q. WHICH PARTY GAME DOES A TORNADO LIKE TO PLAY?   A. TWISTER!

HA HA

Trouble ahead! A menacing, dark column of air reaching from a thundercloud to the ground is the telltale sign of a twister. If you see one coming, get out of the way as fast as you can!

Staying Safe!

Wild weather can kill! Imagine seeing the sky darken. The wind begins to howl, rain lashes down, and suddenly you're fighting for your life! Whatever the weather, there are ways to protect yourself and your property.

High and Dry

In Indonesia, Singapore, and other Pacific regions, people who live by the sea often build their houses on stilts. When floods and storms swamp their villages, they can just pull up the ladders to their homes and stay high and dry.

EXTRA! EXTRA!
After heavy rain in the Atlantic Ocean, a wall of water, called a surge tide, rises up and washes into the North Sea. It could swamp the land and put lives at risk.

Look Behind You!

Tornadoes are tricky to predict. In tornado-prone areas, people build storm cellars under their houses or in their gardens. At the first hint of a twister, people dash for the safety of the cellar.

This barrier across the Thames River protects the city of London, England, from flooding caused by surge tides.

Stone by Stone

In many parts of the world, high walls are built as protection from flooding and surge tides. In some countries, these walls are made from soil. In the Philippines, people build flood walls from rocks and stones.

How
do I stay safe during a thunderstorm?

Move indoors or into your car, if you can. What if you are caught out in the open? Here are a few handy hints.

Move away from open spaces, such as fields or high hillside ridges. If you don't have time to seek shelter, squat down.

Don't stand under a lone tree. A tree has a lot of water in its trunk. If the tree's hit by lightning, the water boils and can make the tree explode.

Desert and Drought

In a desert, the weather is nearly always the same. There are no clouds, so there is no rain — just nonstop sunshine beating down day after day. Although most deserts are hot by day, they are freezing at night. There are no clouds to act as a blanket to keep in heat!

Buried in Sand

In a sandstorm, wind whips sand into the air and carries it in huge, choking clouds that billow along. A car or truck caught in a sandstorm can have its motor clogged, and end up completely buried. Whole villages have even disappeared under sandstorms.

That's Weird!

When the wind blows, a sand dune changes shape and moves around the desert. It shifts up to 1 foot (30 cm) a day, and much more during a sandstorm. It's easy to get lost after a storm as the landscape looks so different!

It didn't look like that last week!

Dreadful Drought

This cracked earth spells disaster. It's a dry field where no crops will grow, due to lack of rain. These conditions are called drought. There are several factors that can lead to drought, but once it starts, the lack of moisture in the soil makes it even harder for clouds to form and rain to occur. Drought is common in parts of Africa.

EXTRA! EXTRA!

A sandstorm can be a wall of dust as much as 5,000 feet (1,525 m) tall. That's as high as a small mountain!

Clothes for the Climate

Tuareg tribespeople live in the biggest desert in the world — the Sahara in Africa. They wear clothes suited to the hot, dry climate. Long, flowing robes keep them cool and protect their skin from the sun. If a sandstorm blows up, they protect their eyes by pulling their headdresses across their faces. But don't worry, they can see through them!

BUMP!

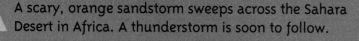

A scary, orange sandstorm sweeps across the Sahara Desert in Africa. A thunderstorm is soon to follow.

HA HA

Snow and Ice

There's a lot of water up in the atmosphere, waiting to fall on your head! Usually, it falls as rain, but when it's extra cold it falls as snow. In bitter, driving wind, a snowfall soon becomes an icy blizzard!

Watch Out!

A hailstone is made when a drop of ice in a thundercloud is tossed up and down. It picks up a coating of water and quickly turns to a hard ball of ice. When a hailstone is too heavy to stay in the cloud, it falls to the ground. Most hailstones are the size of peas, but some can be as big as oranges.

TRUE STORY!

In 1888, during a hailstorm in India, gigantic hailstones the size of basketballs were said to have rained down. Imagine trying to avoid them!

Coming Down

Ice crystals form at the tops of clouds. The crystals join together and form snowflakes that fall through the cloud. They fall faster as they get larger and eventually fall out of the cloud. Mostly, they fall through warm air and turn to rain on the way down.

It's a long way down!

EXTRA! EXTRA

In New York City m
than 2 feet (60 cm
snow can fall in
storm. That's eno
snow to come almost
up to your waist!

Q. WHAT'S A SNOWMAN'S FAVORITE SONG? A. THERE'S NO BUSINESS LIKE SN

HA HA

Imagine coming outside to find your car buried in snow, like this one in New York City!
Snow causes trouble on the roads, so when things get tough, snowplows get going.

Avalanche!

Watch out! It's coming down the mountainside faster than a freight train. Get out of the way or you'll be buried alive by an avalanche!

Q. WHAT DID THE BURIED SNOWBOARDER SAY? A. THERE'S SNOW WAY OUT!

 This avalanche in Mount Rainier National Park, Washington, hurtles down the mountainside at 80 miles per hour (130 kmh). It took just five seconds to reach this speed!

On a Roll

Avalanches happen on mountainsides when snow melts and breaks loose, cascading to the valley below. Many avalanches are caused by skiers and snowboarders disturbing loose snow. Loud noises do not set off avalanches. Low-flying helicopters and sonic booms from aircraft only cause avalanches in movies!

Snow Shooters

To protect villages from avalanches, experts fire missiles from special guns at suspect snow. The missiles cause small explosions that set off harmless mini-avalanches. These stop snow from building up and causing massive destruction.

That's Weird!

You can have a device like a radio sewn into your ski clothes. If you're buried by an avalanche, it sends a signal that helps a rescuer to find you. Otherwise, you could be sniffed out by a type of rescue dog, called a Saint Bernard.

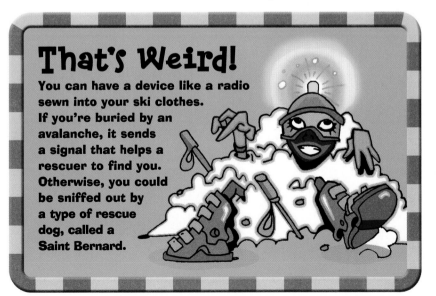

How

do I escape from an avalanche?

If you're caught in an avalanche, try to move off the shifting snow before it picks up speed and carries you away.

Try to grab hold of a tree and then cling on for dear life! If you are lucky, the tree will stay put.

If an avalanche is coming toward you, ski downhill to build up speed, then veer off to the left or right.

Weird Weather

Flying saucers, ghostly ships in the sky, downpours of frogs. Many people believe that they have truly seen such things. But really they are false images created by weird weather. Oh, apart from the rain of frogs — that actually happened!

The shiny UFO in the sky is water vapor! Clouds like this are called lenticular (lens-shaped) clouds. They are found near mountaintops where gusts of wind whip them into shape.

Is that a Ghost?

Nope, it's a mirage! A mirage is an eerie image that appears when light from beyond the horizon bends as it passes through the sky. This happens when warm air sits on top of cold air. Legend has it that a ghost ship, called the *Flying Dutchman*, appears off Africa's southern tip. In reality, ghost ships such as this are probably images of real ships just over the horizon.

Croaking Cloud

In 1939, thousands of frogs rained down on the amazed people of Trowbridge, England. At other times, worms, pebbles, and sheep have also fallen from the sky. What probably happened is that they were picked up by a tornado, whisked up to a thundercloud, then dropped elsewhere in pouring rain.

TRUE STORY!

In June 1996, a blue-and-white ball the size of an orange flew into a factory in England. It zoomed around bumping into machines as astonished workers watched. Then it flew into a window and exploded. What the staff had seen was a very rare type of lightning called ball lightning.

What's in Store?

What will the weather be like tomorrow? Weather forecasting today is a computerized, space-age, high-tech business. But weather changes quickly, so even with the most up-to-date equipment, weather forecasters still get it wrong.

EXTRA! EXTRA!
Weather in Antarctica affects weather conditions in other places around the world. That's why some weather forecasters work here — in the coldest, windiest place on Earth!

Weather forecasting can be hard work! These two scientists have had to put on many layers of clothing before checking their measuring instruments at a weather station in Antarctica.

Weather Gobbler

To forecast the weather, information from weather stations, satellites, weather balloons, planes, and ships all over the world is fed into computers. The computers gobble up this information, then work out what the weather will be like for each place over time. Weather forecasters look at the results and tell us what's going to happen — probably!

That's Weird!

Some pilots are paid to fly planes straight into the middle of fierce thunderstorms! Specially strengthened planes with weather-monitoring equipment fly into the center of lightning storms and hail-filled clouds to research weather conditions.

Up and Away

Once this weather balloon is released into the air, its journey is tracked by computers. The instruments it carries send back readings about wind direction, temperature, and humidity, which is the amount of water in the air. The launcher wears goggles in case the wind blows the balloon and it hits the person in the face.

Extra Amazing

Want to know what's what with the weather? Then look no further. The hottest, coldest, wettest, driest places in the world — they're all here in this sensational guide to the most awe-inspiring weather statistics!

Chill-out Zone

Are you too hot to handle? Then cool your heels in the Antarctic, the world's most teeth-chatteringly freezing-cold spot. English explorer Robert Falcon Scott wrote, "This is an awful place." Temperatures can drop as low as -128°F (-89°C) — that's about 20 times colder than your freezer at home!

Top Hot Spots

Where are things really sizzling? Al'Azīzīyah, Libya, that's where. A world-record temperature of 136.4°F (58°C) was recorded here in 1922. For guaranteed all-year-round heat, try Dallol, Ethiopia, which has the world's highest average daily temperature, at 94°F (34°C). Here, you could fry an egg on a rock!

Dry as a Bone

Calama in the Atacama Desert, Chile, is the driest place on Earth. There was no rain for 400 years until a single downpour occurred in 1971. The rest of the Atacama Desert gets a tiny sprinkle of water from a shower — or a lick of wetness from fog — two or three times every 100 years.

Oh, My Aching Head

Are you uncomfortable in muggy weather? You'd better not live in Tororo, Uganda, then. People here have an average of 250 thunder-filled days a year. That's more than two out of three days when it thunders.

My Thunder Chart

Dreary Downpour

Mount Waialeale on the Hawaiian island of Kauai is the rainiest place on Earth. It rains for a dreary 350 days a year.

Wet All Over

Mawsynram in India is actually the world's wettest place. It has an average annual rainfall of 467 inches (1,186 cm). Imagine having about 30 tubs of water poured over your head!

UMBRELLAS!

True or False?

Are you a weather whiz-kid? Test your knowledge and say whether each of these is true or false. Answers are on page 32, but no cheating!

1. Avalanches happen when snow freezes to ice.

2. Houses on stilts keep their owners safe from high winds.

3. Lightning is hotter than the sun's surface.

4. This is a picture of a hurricane.

5. Monsoon rains are common in North America.

6. The middle of a hurricane is called the eye.

Weather Terms

air current
A steady flow of air in one particular direction.

atmosphere
A layer of gases around a planet.

blizzard
A mix of heavy snowfall, low temperature, and high wind that makes it hard to see in front of you.

climate
The weather in an area over a long period of time.

cloud
Large amounts of water particles in the sky, which form a fine white or gray mist.

cumulonimbus
A large, tall cloud that makes hail, thunder, and lightning. Cumulonimbus clouds are the largest clouds of all.

drought
A long period of time when there is no rainfall.

fog
A thick mist caused by water particles. Fog is similar to a cloud but occurs on the ground.

hailstones
Balls of ice that fall from clouds. Hailstones are usually about the size of frozen peas.

7 Weather reports are 100% accurate.

8 A waterspout is a tornado that forms over a sea or lake.

9 Climate is another name for weather.

10 This is one of the most dangerous places you can stand during a thunderstorm.

11 Deserts are the result of too much rain.

12 In the world's monsoon regions, there are four seasons.

13 Hailstones are frozen pebbles sucked up by tornadoes.

14 There was once a downpour of frogs.

15 Avalanches can travel at 80 miles per hour (130 kmh).

16 Tornado Alley is in Canada.

17 Soil, methane gas, and moonlight are the three essential ingredients of weather.

18 Lightning is caused by thunder.

19 Most weather happens in the lowest part of the atmosphere.

20 The shape of this cloud is called lenticular.

---

humidity
The amount of water in the air.

hurricane
A huge storm that starts out at sea. Hurricanes are most common in the tropics.

lightning
A bolt of electricity formed in a thundercloud, which shoots between clouds or from a cloud to the ground.

monsoon
A wind that brings very heavy rain to India and Southeast Asia.

season
A period of change in the weather, such as winter, that happens every year.

thunder
A loud rumbling sound heard after a lightning flash. It happens because lightning makes gases in the atmosphere expand.

tornado
A spinning column of air, hanging from a thundercloud to the ground.

tropics
Regions of the world near the equator.

troposphere
The lowest part of the atmosphere, where most of the world's weather happens.

water vapor
A gas that forms when water from a sea, a river, or a lake is heated by the sun.

Index

Answers

1	False	11	False
2	False	12	False
3	True	13	False
4	False	14	True
5	False	15	True
6	True	16	False
7	False	17	False
8	True	18	False
9	False	19	True
10	True	20	True

Author: Paul Dowswell
Illustrations: Stuart Harrison
Consultant: Helen Young, BBC Weather Centre
Photographs: Cover: Craig Aurness/CORBIS; p. 2 Tony Stone Images; pp. 4-5 CORBIS/The Stock Market/Stocktrek; p. 7 Johnny Autrey/Science Photo Library; p. 8 Reuters NewMedia Inc. /CORBIS; p. 9 Jim Sugar Photography/CORBIS; pp. 10-11 Tony Stone Images; p. 12 Raymond Gehman/CORBIS; p. 13 Tony Arruza /CORBIS; p. 15 Warren Faidley/Oxford Scientific Films; p. 16 Pictor Uniphoto; pp. 16-17 Pictor Un   ɔ; pp. 18-19 Grant McDowell/BBC Natural History Unit; p. 19 Ɩ ɔce Coleman Inc.; p. 20 Tony Stone Images; p. 21 Tony Stone Images; p. 22 Tony Stone Images; pp. 24-25 Doug Allan/BBC Natural History Unit; p. 26 NHPA/Rich Kirchner; p. 27 Roger Garwood & Trish Ainslie /CORBIS; p. 28 David Tipling/BBC Natural History Unit; pp. 28-29 Jaime Plaza Van Roon/Ardea London.

Created by **act-two** for Scholastic Inc. Copyright © **act-two**, 2001 All rights reserved. Published by Scholastic Inc.

SCHOLASTIC and associated logos are trademarks and/or registered trademarks of Scholastic Inc.

ISBN 0-439-28602-6

12 11 10 9 8 7 6 5 4 3 2 1   1 2 3 4 5 6/0

Printed in the U.S.A.

First Scholastic printing, September 2001